Wax Sculpturing

The modeling of wax as outlined in this book is just a start, an introductory offer, so to speak, into a field of sculpture that is immediate, inventive and creative.

Wax is a plastic and needs only a slight warming to become malleable. It is a medium in which great detail and movement can be portrayed. Wax can be reshaped, twisted and retwisted without breaking or falling apart, so that if you make a mistake, it can be corrected with no trouble and no one the wiser. Even in the hands of the amateur, surprising results can be achieved by simply modeling the wax with thumb and fingers alone. It is a clean material and can be carried in the pocket to work on whenever you want. There's nothing to stop you from modeling a figure while you are riding on a bus or subway. Chances are, by the time you reach your destination you will have finished a piece.

Nature offers fine sculptural material in the golden-brown wax that bees use to build their honeycombs. Therefore it seems as natural as the material itself that modeling in wax is one of the oldest sculptural mediums known to man. Wax sculpturing was practiced several centuries before Christ and was worked in various ways. The result was either used as a model for casting statues and other objects or as a finished piece in itself, for although waxes are fragile and subject to heat and cold, they can last forever if not melted or mishandled.

The earliest records we have are Egyptian sculptures, such as the miniature wax head done in 700 B.C. The Egyptians not only modeled three dimensional pieces, they also painted by means of wax combined with color. The colors became fixed when fused with hot irons, and the method is known as encaustic painting. The portrait of an Egyptian boy was done in the second century A.D. by this method and is still in fine condition.

The Greeks made gods for their religious ceremonies and fashioned dolls of wax for their children to play with. The Romans modeled wax masks of their ancestors. It was during the Renaissance in Italy that sculpturing with wax was developed into a highly refined art. Benvenuto Cellini, famous as a goldsmith and sculptor, was undoubtedly a leader in the revival of this ancient craft. He, as well as other artists, used the material for designing plaques, medals, cups and jewelry. It is supposed that Cellini used beeswax alone, but most artists had their own secret formulas. Some used white, while others used colored waxes.

The incomparable Leonardo da Vinci, who was an inventor as well as painter and sculptor, also worked in wax. This model, which is still in existence, was a study for the equestrian statue of Francesco Sforza. It is known as the *cavallino* or "little horse."

Before the Spaniards ever landed in the Americas, the Aztecs as well as other Indian tribes were expert goldsmiths and had developed a method of casting, using gold and other metals, without any influence from the old world or other civilizations. Pictured on the next page are a 16th century pre-Columbian rattle and a pendant made from wax and cast in gold.

Miniature Wax Head
Philadelphia Museum of Art
Photograph by A. J. Wyatt,
Staff Photographer

Portrait of an Egyptian Boy
The Metropolitan Museum of Art
Rogers Fund, 1909

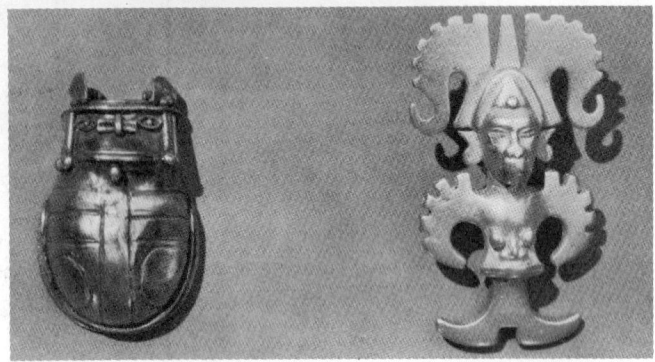

Pre-Columbian Rattle and Pendant *The Museum of Primitive Art*

On another continent the Beni of Nigeria in Africa also did remarkable work. They made figures and useful objects as well as jewelry. They also devised a means to cast a permanent piece from a wax model. They too were a self-contained people who did not have book, teacher or any knowledge of art or the world beyond their own borders. The object below is an example of Benin sculpture.

The University Museum, University of Pennsylvania

It is quite common for most people to associate wax with a waxworks rather than a medium for the sculptor, and waxworks seems to be synonymous with Mme. Tussaud's, which is still a tourist attraction in London. Mme. Tussaud, who lived during the time of Louis XVI, was a teacher to Louis's sister, Elizabeth. Her career as a sculptress had a gruesome beginning, for she was forced to make death masks of some of the victims of the terror during the French revolution. She was finally permitted to leave France, and she went to London, where she modeled the more fortunate heads of people of renown, which eventually led her to establish the waxworks. Pictured above right are models of Charles Dickens and Somerset Maugham which are in Madame Tussaud's waxworks; the photograph is courtesy of Madame Tussaud's Ltd.

Gutzon Borglum, the American sculptor, whose monumental heads of presidents adorn Mount Rushmore, also excelled in wax. The fine bust of George Washington pictured here is an example of his work.

Jewelers use wax for many of their models. The mouse paperweight, which is two inches tall, was fashioned in wax and cast in silver.

Bust of George Washington
The Metropolitan Museum of Art
Gift of Henry L. Moses, 1958

Mouse Paperweight
Photograph courtesy of Tiffany & Co.

In recent years more and more sculptors have turned to wax to work with rather than clay, plasticene or other sculpture media. They found that wax was a more fluid means of expression, permitting greater scope and minute refinement. Wax responds with an immediacy that catches a mood and movement, putting life into the piece. The following sculptures were done by Frank Eliscu.

2 *Wax*

WORKING WITH WAX

The would-be sculptor doesn't have to invent a secret formula anymore because beeswax can be bought at any dime, hobby or art supply store. However, all the projects in this book were modeled with inexpensive synthetic wax, which is the color and consistency of beeswax. It comes in blocks of soft, medium or hard; medium is recommended for the beginner.

The sculptures below were done with synthetic wax by a fifteen-year-old pupil in the High School of Art and Design in New York City.

To work with wax you need only your fingers and a sharpened pencil. The pencil is used for modeling faces or for pressing parts to join them to the piece you are working on. You may also find it helpful to use a knife to cut the wax, a candle for heat to fuse pieces together, and a spoon to achieve rounded effects.

The wax techniques are simple. You can pinch, stretch or twist a piece of wax into a desired shape and then add rolls, coils or pellets to build up the figure. To join one piece of wax to another you simply apply pressure.

Wax can be softened by warming the material in the palm of the hand. It can be put in the sun for a short time or placed on a piece of paper on a radio, television set or near the warmth of a radiator until it is the right consistency. If the wax gets too oozy or soft, put it in a cool place for a few moments. If the wax you are working should crack, it means it wasn't warm enough, but this is no problem. Work the wax with your fingers and it will soften. If your fingers feel sticky when you have finished working, wash your hands with water and any powdered household detergent.

Let's begin with a very simple sculpture.

TURTLE

You need a lump of softened wax, a sharpened pencil, a knife and a spoon.

To make a thin shell for the turtle's back, first wet the spoon. If the spoon is dry, you will have a hard time removing the wax, but wax will not stick to a wet surface and the shell will slip out freely from a moistened spoon.

1. Press a small piece of wax onto the spoon.

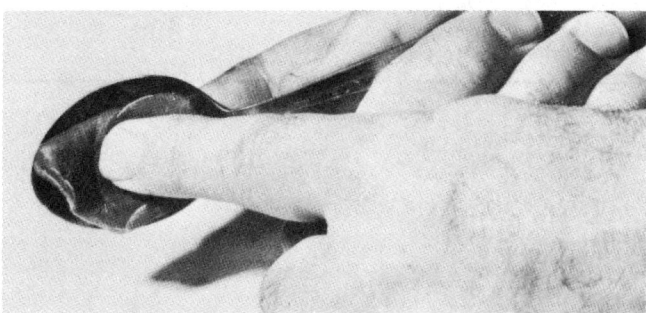

2. Trim the excess wax from around the edges of the spoon with a knife.

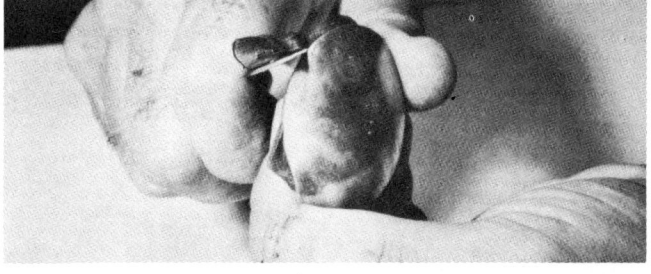

3. Slip the wax shell from the spoon.

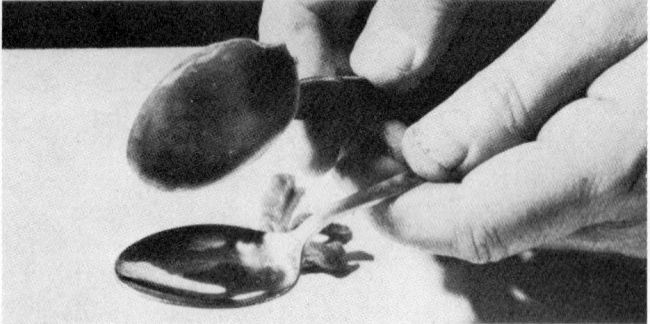

4. Roll a small piece of wax in the palms of your hands. Shape it into an S and press it to the shell for the turtle's head.

5. Make the turtle's legs by rolling four very small pieces of wax and attaching them to the underside of the turtle shell, front and back.

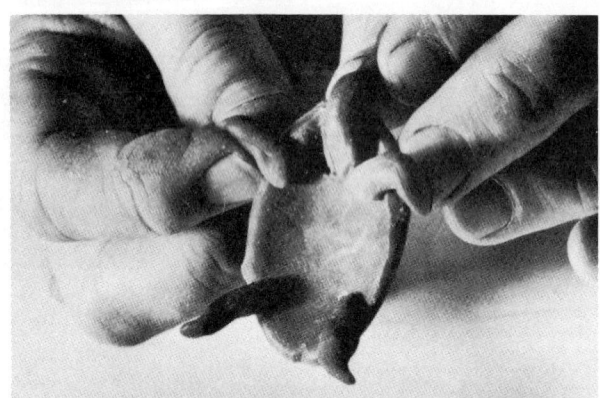

6. Press a tiny bit of wax under the back of the shell for the tail. Incise markings on the turtle's back with a sharpened pencil.

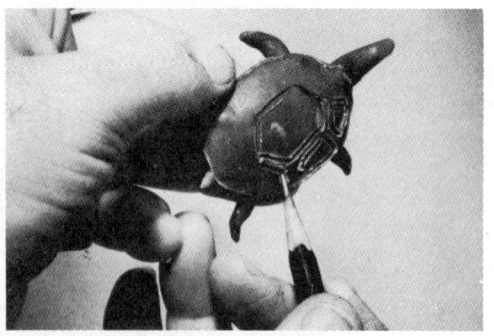

7. Make eyes by digging the point of the pencil into both sides of the head. (Be sure to moisten the pencil so that the wax doesn't stick to the pencil point.) Indent lines with the pencil around the neck and legs of the turtle for wrinkles.

8. Mount the turtle on a stone.

9. If you want a whole turtle, make another thin shell of wax smaller than the first, using the spoon as a mold. Slip the shell from the spoon. Incise four lines on the stomach with the pencil. Press the stomach to the underside of the shell, and your piece has "turned turtle."

4 Wax

FISH

In this next sculpture some drippings from a candle suggested an unusual base. The materials you'll need are a lump of clay, a pencil, a retractable ball-point pen, a knife and a candle.

1. Roll a piece of wax into a cigar shape.

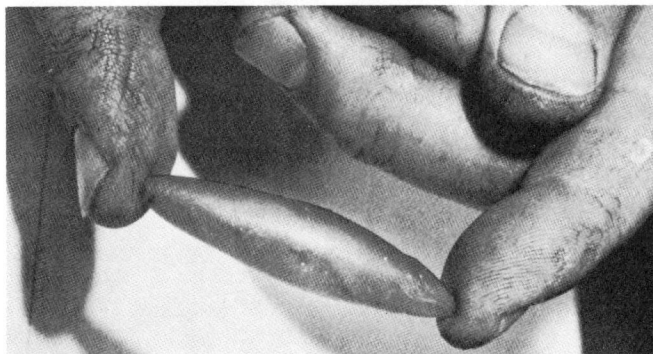

2. Flatten the cigar shape between the heels of your hands.

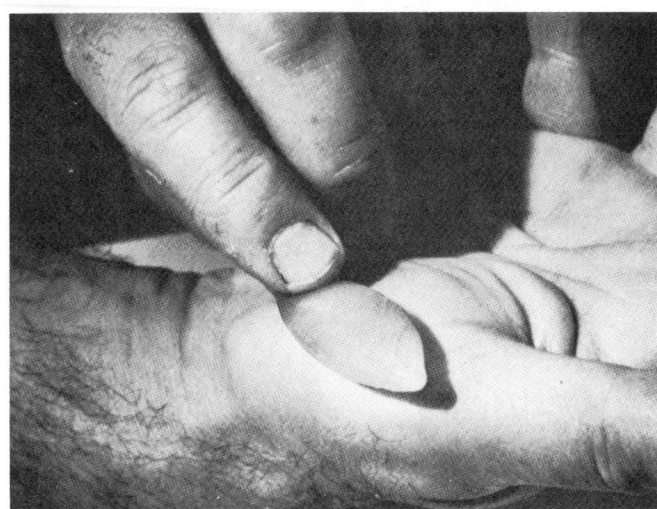

3. Roll two tiny pieces of wax into miniature cigars and attach them to the front of the fish to form the mouth.

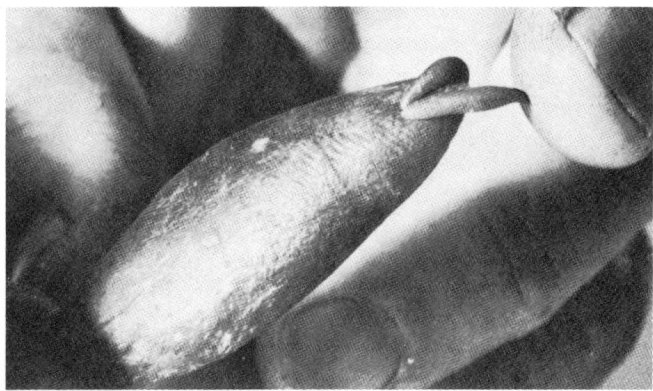

4. With the pencil dig a line down the middle of the fish and a curved line at the head for the gill. Press the end of the fish with your fingers so that the wax flares into a tail. Wet the end of the ball-point pen and press into the sides of the head for eyes. Lightly press the retracted ball-point pen on the upper back of the fish for spots.

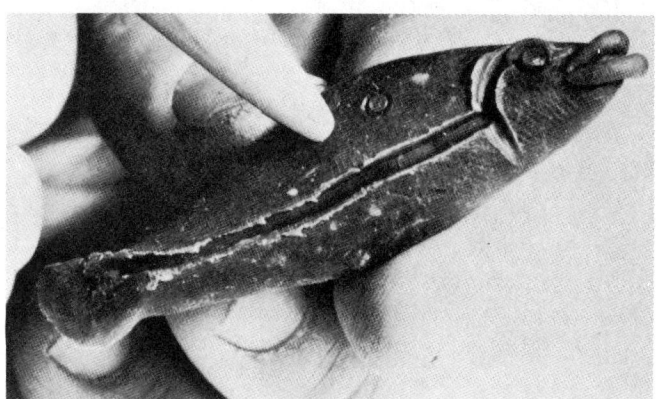

5. Allow the wax from a lit candle to drip in a triangular pile, forming the base. Press the fish to the top of the base. For a sea sponge, shape a small roll of wax; press the point of a pencil into the top of the roll to open it and give it a tubelike effect. The sea sponge is a fragile form and will lose its shape if pressed to the base. Heat the blade of a knife in a candle flame and touch the tip of the sea sponge to melt a drop of hot wax; attach lightly to the base. The piece will adhere when the wax hardens.

6. Shape a few more sea sponges and attach and fuse them to the base. Open the fish's mouth with the knife. Curve the body of the fish to denote a swimming action.

Wax

Twist the tail and add a few markings to the tail with the pencil. Mount the base on a sea shell.

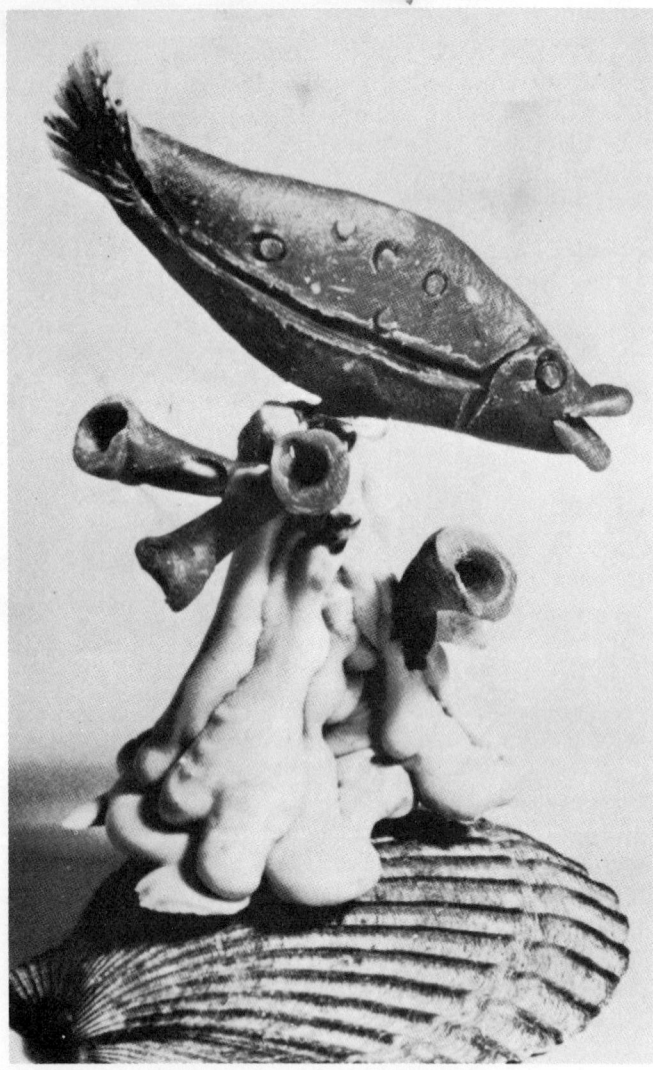

2. Add a tiny piece of wax in the shape of a triangle to make the head and a tinier piece for the tail.

3. Bend the wings of the birds upward with your fingers. Press one bird to the other, wing to wing, to create a composition of a flock of birds in flight.

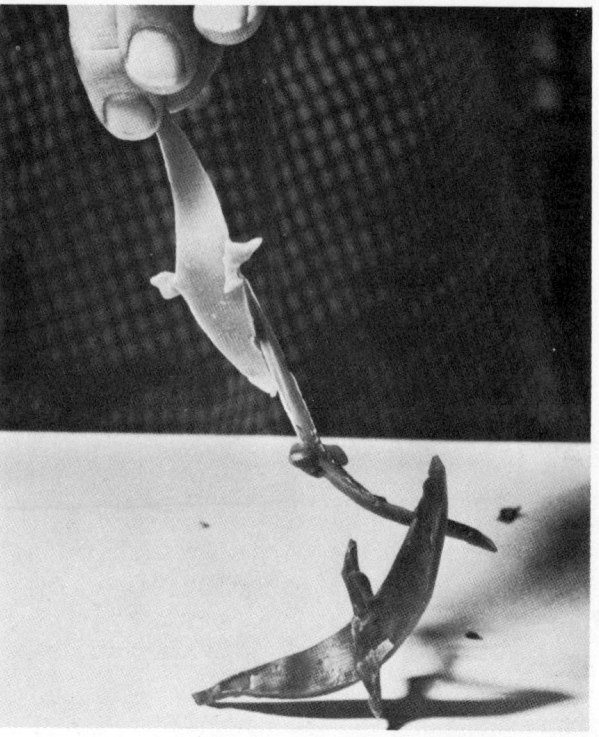

FLIGHT

The following piece may seem complicated because several figures are involved, but this interesting composition can be modeled very easily. You need a chunk of wax, a knife, a candle, a block of wood and florist's wire.

1. Cut thin slivers of wax approximately ⅛ inch in thickness, or less, in the shape of triangles. Cut a rough shape of birds with their wings outspread.

4. Press a blob of wax onto a wooden block and stick wires into the wax; attach the birds to the wires. Melt a drop of wax on the tip of the knife and fuse the wings to join the birds to each other.

5. Stick more pieces of wire into wax blobs on the base, attach more birds to the wires and then fuse them.

ABSTRACTS

Imaginations can often take flight in doing an abstract. In the following example, forms are used like an erector set. No modeling or pressing is necessary. Wax, a candle, a knife and a piece of wire are needed.

1. Cut strips of wax with a knife in various thicknesses and shapes. Move various shapes around until you get a composition that interests you. Fuse the pieces one to the other with a hot knife blade.

2. Heat the end of a piece of wire in the candle flame and make holes in the wax. Add textures by wetting the knife and impressing the point of the knife into the wax, or make any pattern or design that will add interest to the piece. Wet the pencil point or ball-point pen and incise or press circles. Experiment with a shell, a bit of coral, a fork or anything that will make an impression; wet the object and press it into the piece.

3. Some of the methods employed for the abstract were used in modeling this fawn.

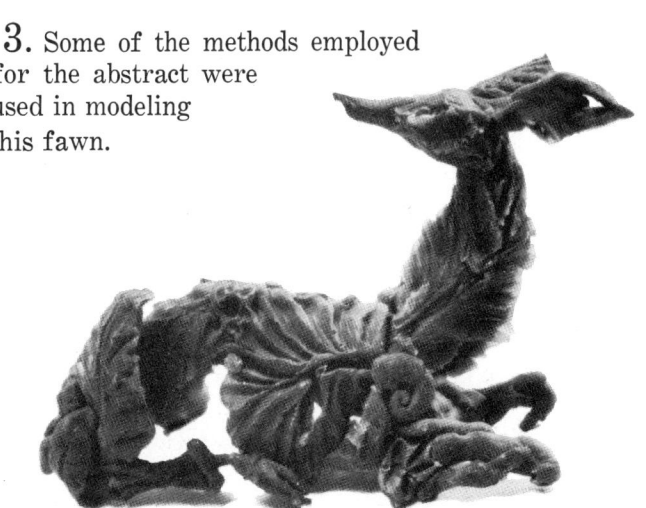

Wax 7

GREYHOUND

Most people love dogs; it would be fun to sculpt one's own pet. Here is an Italian greyhound to practice on. When you have become more proficient with wax, you can use your own dog as a model. Wax, a knife and a pencil are all that are necessary to model this figure.

1. Roll a piece of softened wax into a cigar shape. Stretch the front part a little for the head. Cut out a piece of wax from the center back of the cigar shape for the dog's chest (below left).

2. Refine the head, using your fingers to draw the dog's muzzle forward. The greyhound looks something like a sea horse at this stage of work (below right).

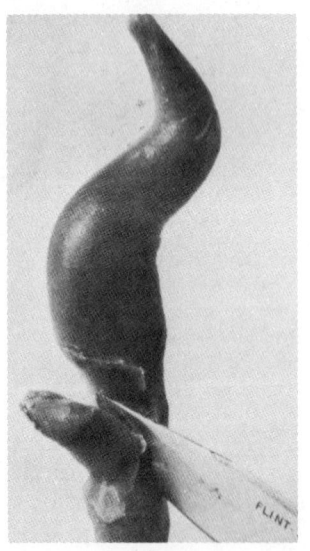
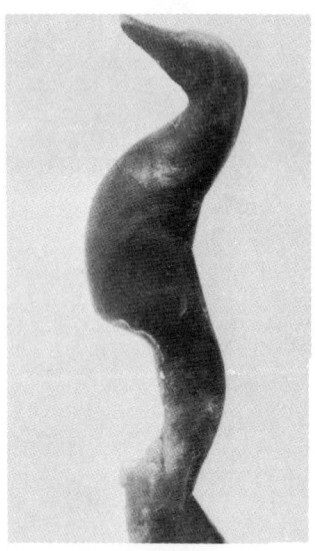

5. Thin the neck by paring the excess wax with the knife. This gives a better proportion and indicates the shoulder muscles of the body.

6. Cut and model two pieces of wax for the forelegs. Fill out the body and chest by adding wax pellets. Add a tail by rolling a piece of wax into a long, thin, rounded piece. Make the eyes with a pencil point.

3. Cut into the back of the head with the knife to make ears.

4. Model the ears. Cut two pieces of wax for the back legs and model them with your fingers (above right).

The figure of the dog can be made to do tricks by changing its position. In order to do so, you must be sure to bend the body at the joints. If you try to change a leg or shoulder by bending it any which way except at the joints, you will end up with limbs that look like boiled macaroni. If you do change the figure's position, be sure to press either side of the joint gently. This will hold the form of the figure while you are working on it.

8 *Wax*

Twist the body so that the dog is in a reclining position.

Make him retrieve.

Good boy!

HORSE

Sculptors have always found the modeling of horses and the human figure to be the greatest challenge. But in the following pieces the approach is so simplified that a good result can be obtained simply by following directions. As your skills develop, so will your figures.

Flatten a piece of wax to about 1/8 inch in thickness with a rolling pin, being sure to dampen the surface of the table or board you are working on. Bend the flattened piece of wax into a curved piece. This will be the horse's blanket.

1. With a small piece of wax, model a horse's head as well as you can, using your fingers to shape the head and neck. Add a small piece of wax to the neck for the part of the body that will go under the horse's blanket. Roll two tiny pellets of wax for ears and shape and attach them to the head. Model two forelegs and two hind legs from strips of wax and shape the hoofs with your fingers. Roll a piece of wax between the palms of your hands for the tail.

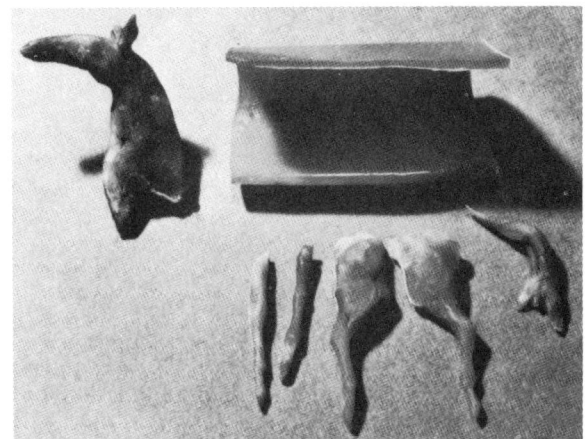

2. Press the head under the front of the blanket. Press the legs in place. Push out the sides of the blanket to indicate the stomach of the horse. Push the back of the blanket down on the hindquarters to follow the horse's shape. Refer to the photograph on the next page.

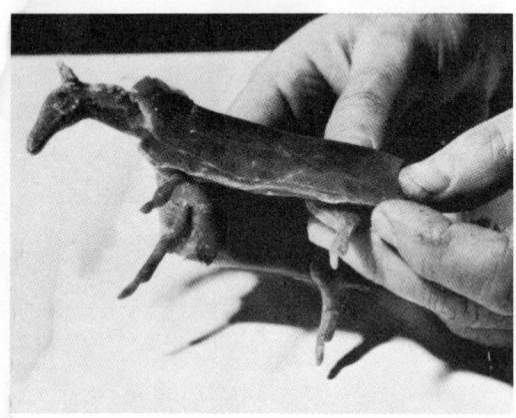

3. Adjust the legs to achieve the desired action. Push a hole into the back of the blanket with a pencil and insert the tail into the hole. Make eyes with the pencil point. Add a bit of wax for a forelock between the ears.

4. Add a piece of wax to the neck for the mane. Make lines with the pencil to indicate hair on the forelock, mane and tail. Model the horse's head and legs with your fingers or a sharpened pencil and add muscles with pellets of wax. Open the mouth with the knife.

Here is a jousting horse modeled in wax and a finished piece cast in bronze beside it. Make a curved piece for the horse's blanket. Stretch this piece longer than the one for the horse you have just completed. Model the head, tail and the forelegs only. Attach the head and push out the sides of the blanket. Press the forelegs into place and adjust the legs upward and outward for a rearing action.

FIGURES

Before we start to do a human figure, it is important to remember that when you wish to change the position of your piece, bend the body at the joints, such as the knee, ankle, elbow etc., and press both sides of the joint so that your figure will hold its shape.

1. Roll out a conical shape of wax for the trunk of the body. Roll out two smaller cone-shaped pieces for the legs, making the tops thicker than the bottoms. Roll out two smaller and thinner conical shapes (again, from thick to thin) for the arms. Form a piece of wax into an egg shape for the head. Be sure the size of the egg is in proportion to the body. Shape both ends of the trunk to slope the neck and pelvic areas. Press the head to the neck. Press the arms and legs to the trunk.

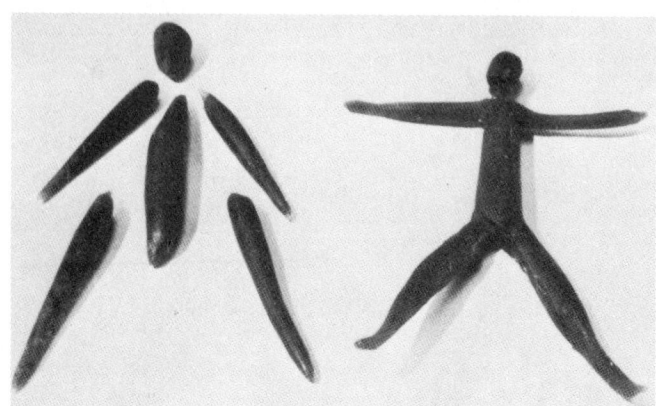

2. Refine the figure, turning it into a male acrobat with well-developed muscles. Make the shoulders wider and fill out the chest and the seat by adding pellets of wax.

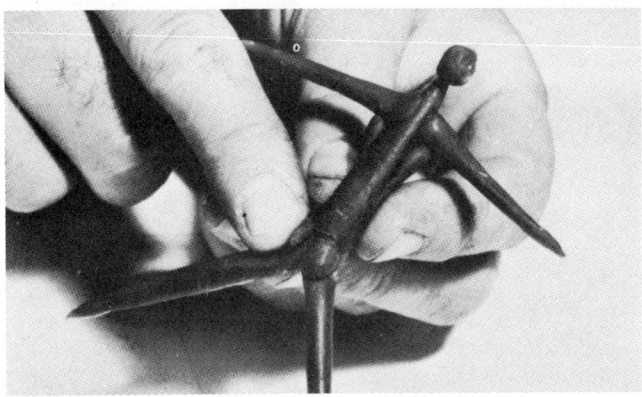

3. Make a line for swim trunks with a pencil. Bend the feet at the ankle joints and the hands at the wrists. Balance the acrobat on one hand.

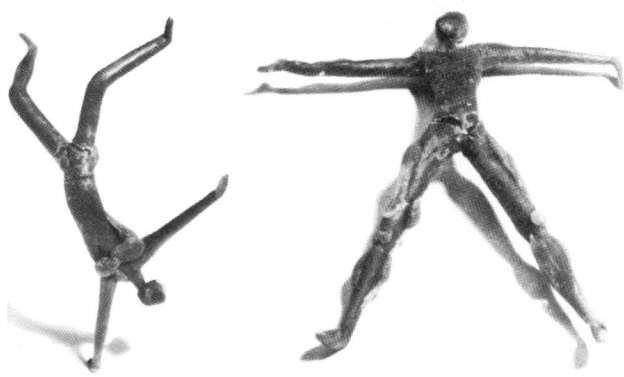

4. The figure will maintain its position because wax has such tensile strength that it can be balanced without the support of an armature or any support such as wood, metal rods, etc. By experimenting with this same basic figure, you can turn it into a skier, a football player, a dancer and so on.

5. Further delineate key points of the male figure, such as the knee cap, thigh muscles, etc., by adding pellets of wax (above right).

6. The female figure (below left) is made exactly as the male (below right). Add form to the chest area and pellets of wax for the hip area.

CIRCUS CAROUSEL

Combining the horse and the two figures results in an interesting composition. Roll a long piece of wax for a pole, thicker at the base, and fuse to the horse's back. Attach the male figure to the horse's back with his hand on the pole.

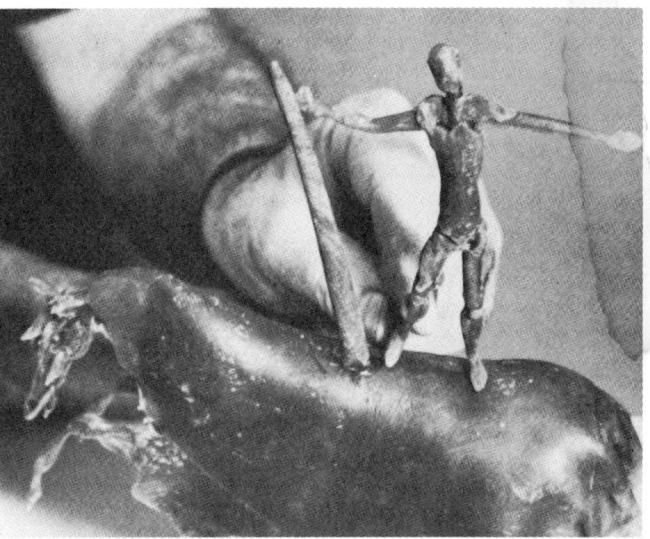

Attach the female figure facing in the opposite direction and fuse the figures.

A finished piece need not be rough. The wax can be blended into a smooth, flat surface. But when a textured piece is cast, the bronze or other metal will have greater excitement and appear livelier because of the variation of rough and smooth and the contrast of highlight and shadow.

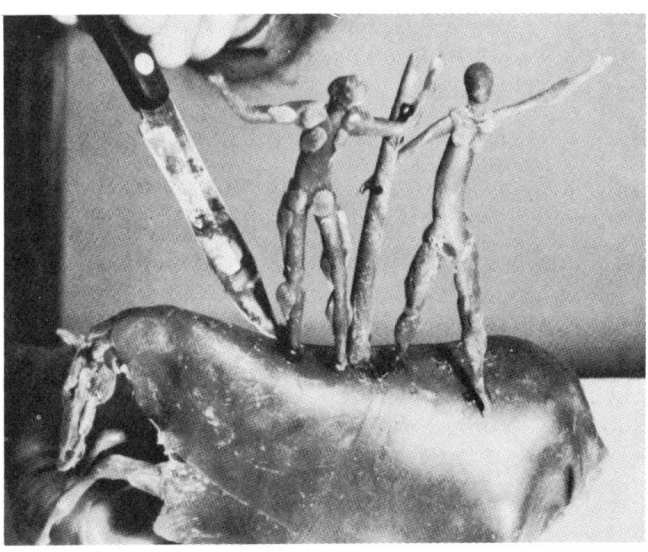

Wax 11

A wax sculpture can be kept indefinitely if given proper care. It can be painted or sprayed. (Don't use a paint mixed with turpentine, for turpentine cuts wax.) You can shellac the piece and then color it with gold, copper or bronze powder, or you can use a clear lacquer spray and then paint any part that you wish to stand out with oil colors.

If you have modeled a piece that you really believe is outstanding or that you just want as a keepsake, you can have the figure cast in metal. Casting is not inexpensive, however, and it is wise to keep practicing your skills as a sculptor before you decide to cast a work for posterity.

Artists in the past had to use gelatin, wet clay, fireproof material, tubes and metal rods and all sorts of paraphernalia to get a cast. Today this work is done in a similar but less complicated fashion in the foundry. Very few sculptors today do their own casting. The necessary equipment is expensive, although with the modern invention of centrifugal machinery the process has become enormously simplified.

Cire perdue or lost wax method is what is used in casting wax. The French word *cire* means "wax," and *perdue* means "lost." The object to be cast is placed in a drum (a metal container) that has a hole in the bottom. A plaster-like mixture is poured over the object. The drum is placed in an oven. The wax melts and runs out through the hole. Now one has a mold of the object. Hot metal is then literally shot into the mold and takes the exact shape of the original wax object by being spun in a simple centrifuge.

Here is a bronze cast of "Circus Carousel" that was done with the *cire-perdue* method.

Wax is a joy for an artist to work with. It is sensitive yet strong. It will adhere to itself with the slightest pressure at even the tiniest point of contact. It can be stretched, bent, cut apart and put together again with heat, and no matter how roughly it is handled or how much it is worked, it will always retain its purity of form.

Sand Sculpturing

Sand sculpture is fun to do and as easy to make as mud pies.

If you follow the simple step-by-step directions which are given in this book, you will get "molds" that make fine decorations. The only thing left to your imagination will be your own original design or composition. Everything else will be outlined for you, and the many photographs will show you exactly how a sand sculpture or a sand mold is made.

You can make any design that takes your fancy. Your tools are any object that you can lay your hands on. In fact your hands and fingers are tools as well.

You will find tools in the kitchen. For instance, you can use forks, spoons, glasses, potato mashers, etc. The sewing box is filled with tools: spools of thread, a darning egg, scissors, a thimble, and so on. The tool chest has screw drivers, hammers, nails, pliers, etc. In a school, your tools may be pencils, compasses, paste pots, rulers, or the back of an old blackboard eraser. In other words, any object that has a form or shape is a "tool."

To make a sand sculpture, all you need are tools, a box of wet sand, and a bag of plaster.

All you have to do is to scoop or press your design into the wet sand and then cover the sand with plaster. In less time than it takes to make or bake a pie you can see your results. In a little more than an hour you have a piece of art ready to hang or display.

All your materials and tools should be at hand when you work. You also need a place to work. Any flat surface will do. At home or in the classroom you can use tables or desks or the drainboard on the kitchen sink. You also need water. The water is used to wet the sand and also to mix with the plaster that is used when the design is done.

If you are lucky enough to be at the seashore, you don't need a worktable. Then the work can be done right in the sand on the beach. More will be said about this later.

Sand belongs on a beach or in a fish tank or, in this case, in a box, not on the floor or in the soup. It is best to cover your work area with old newspapers or some covering so that the sand doesn't fly about or scatter. Plastic covers that come from the dry cleaners are useful. These make a good protective covering. There needn't be any sand in the scrambled eggs or any mess if you work carefully.

You will notice that there is no protective covering on the work area in the photographs that follow. The covering has been omitted here in order to be sure to give good, clear pictures.

MATERIALS

You will need sand, plaster, a box, strong cord, a bowl, an old toothbrush or soft brush and water.

Any kind of sand will do for your sand sculpture. The next time you go to the beach you can bring home a boxful of it. If you cannot get beach sand, you can buy play sand at toy stores or in any pet shop.

There are many grades of sand, some fine, some coarse. You can use either. If you prefer a fine surface, use fine sand, which will give the sculpture a flat look. If you would rather have a rougher, more textured effect, you should use coarse sand.

Pet shops carry several grades for fish tanks. Four pounds of sand will fill an ordinary cigar box. You can re-use the sand for several molds since only a small amount of it sticks to the plaster when your sculpture is done.

Plaster can be bought in any hardware store. I use plaster of Paris. A five-pound bag will make at least four small molds (cigar or shoe box sizes).

Any box of any size or shape will do for your sculpture. I find cigar boxes best, for they are usually made of thin wood or heavy cardboard that give support to the mold and won't buckle when the plaster is poured. You can get cigar boxes from any cigar or drugstore. They are usually happy to save them and give them away. However, any cardboard box that isn't too flimsy will make a good mold. You can use shoe boxes, tie boxes, scarf boxes, and so on.

You need a strong piece of cord to be used for the "picture hook."

The bowl is needed for mixing plaster.

The soft brush is used for brushing excess sand from the sculpture after it has been "turned out."

TOOLS

Any object that has shape or form can be used: hands, fingers, spatulas, water glasses, jars, bottle tops, spoons, forks, figurines, rulers, compasses, pencils, scissors, thimbles, spools of thread, pliers, screwdrivers, nails, or whatever else you can find around the house.

There are some "extras" you can use in the sculptures. You may want to use shells, beads, stones, bits of wire, or wood in your design. For instance, to make a fish's eye, you can press a bead into the sand for the eye instead of pressing the shape of the eye into the sand with a tool.

TECHNIQUE

Making a sand sculpture is really very simple.

1. Pour the sand into the box.

Fill the box with sand, leaving ½ inch of space at top of the box. This ½ inch is for your plaster backing.

 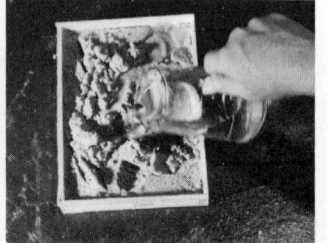

2. Wet the sand thoroughly.

Mix the water and sand together. The sand must be wet but still firm. If the sand is too dry, it will not keep an impression. If the sand is too wet, your impressions will break down.

Always remember to work in firm sand, not *dry*, not *puddly*. But be sure the sand is saturated.

3. Level the sand by smoothing it with your hand or with a spatula or with a plasterer's scraper until you have an even surface.

4. Make the "picture hook."

Take a piece of cord and tie two strong knots, one on each end of it. If you are using a cigar box for the mold, you will need a piece of cord about two inches long. Put the picture hook aside until you are ready for it.

5. Have the bowl and the bag of plaster on the table ready to mix.

Have the tools on the table ready for use.

If you intend to use shells, beads, stones, bits of wire or wood as part of your design, have those at hand also.

Everything is ready but your idea for a composition. It is good to think out a design before starting your sculpture. If you can draw, make a sketch of your composition on a piece of paper, and then work it in the sand.

This isn't necessary, however. You don't have to know anything about drawing. You can work directly in the sand from an idea in your head. If you wish, you can experiment with various "tools." You can do several designs until you get one that pleases you. The nicest part of working in sand is that you can erase out any design until you have found one that you like. Then, pour the plaster and preserve your design.

It is a good idea to make your first mold an experiment. In this way you will learn to mix plaster and become familiar with the simple means of casting in the sand.

It is also important to remember not to press or dig too deeply into the sand. If you do dig to the bottom of the box, the plaster will run through and spoil the effect of your sculpture. Remember, you don't want a plaster cast, you want a sand cast.

HAND CAST

Press your own hand into the box of wet sand.

Make a deep impression of your hand. Remove your hand carefully so that the print is set firmly and clearly outlined.

Your design is ready. Now you will cast your design.

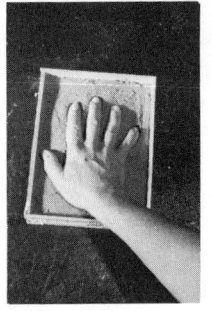  

HOW TO MIX PLASTER

Pour water into a bowl. Add plaster. *Never put plaster into bowl first for it will not mix properly.*

You need about ⅓ more plaster than water. If you use 3 cups of water, you will need 4 to 4½ cups of plaster. Your mixture is ready when the plaster and water look and feel like heavy cream.

This cigar box used for the hand cast measures 2½ inches high, 6½ inches wide, and 8 inches long. For this size box we use 2 measuring cups of water and 2½ to 3 cups of plaster.

(If the mixture is too thin, add a little more plaster until you get the "heavy cream.")

Stir the water and plaster at once and be sure there are no lumps in the mixture. Plaster must be used at once, for it sets fast.

If your plaster gets too thick and starts to harden, throw it away, for it will not pour. You cannot thin the plaster with water. Start fresh and make a new batch.

Take a small amount of plaster and carefully dribble it onto your sand design. Dribble the plaster into the deeper impressions first, then cover the rest of the surface of sand with plaster.

Never pour your plaster directly from the bowl.

Plaster is heavy and will break down the impressions you have made if you do not dribble the first layer into those impressions carefully at first.

When you have covered your design with a thin first layer of plaster (make sure all the impressions are filled), you may then pour the rest of the plaster from the bowl into the box, until the plaster fills the ½ inch space you have allowed for your backing.

Level the plaster so that you have a flat backing using a spatula, plasterer's tool, or your own hand.

If you haven't mixed enough plaster to fill your mold, don't worry. As long as you have covered your design with the first layer, you can mix another batch of plaster and pour it into your mold.

While the plaster is still soft, carefully place the knotted cord or "picture hook" into the plaster. Center the cord so that when your mold is turned out, the sculpture will hang straight. Do not dig the cord too deeply into the plaster for you might break through to your sand design.

It takes approximately one hour for a small mold to set. The plaster will harden almost immediately and will feel cold to the touch. In about a half-hour the

  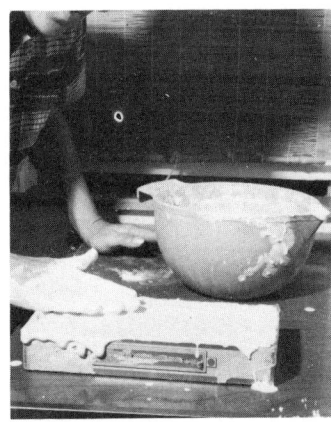 

Sand 15

plaster feels warm. Then it turns cold once again. In an hour you can "turn out" your mold.

Pry off one side of the box. If you are using a cardboard box, you can peel off one side. Now pry off the other three sides of the box.

Carefully lift your mold out. Turn it over and place it on the table. Don't be disappointed if all you see is a square of wet sand. Let your mold dry for another half-hour.

Most of the sand you have used will remain in the bottom of the box from which you have removed the sides. Since the sand was saturated, it will not crumble or fall away. Any sand that does scatter will land on the paper, table, or protective covering and can be cleaned when you are through working. The sand can be used again. Place the remaining sand into a box for future use.

Your sand sculpture is now dry enough for you to brush. Gently brush the surface to remove excess sand. This sand isn't sticking to your plaster backing. As you brush, your design will begin to appear.

Sand sculpture actually consists of nine parts plaster to one part sand. Only a small amount of sand sticks to the plaster.

After you have brushed your mold a few times, you will notice that only a few grains will come off. You have brushed enough and your sand sculpture is finished. Don't be alarmed if sand keeps falling when you touch your sculpture. You won't miss those grains,

and after a while when the mold is thoroughly dried out, not a grain will fall.

Although your sculpture is finished, it is wise to let it dry out for several days before hanging. The plaster will then dry out thoroughly. Your mold will become much lighter in weight when all the moisture from the plaster has evaporated. You will also notice that the sand will lighten in color and take on its permanent value.

You have made your first sculpture. It was an exercise, just for fun and an exercise to make you familiar with your materials. You might want to save the first mold of your hand just as the famous movie stars do. But let us consider it an exercise.

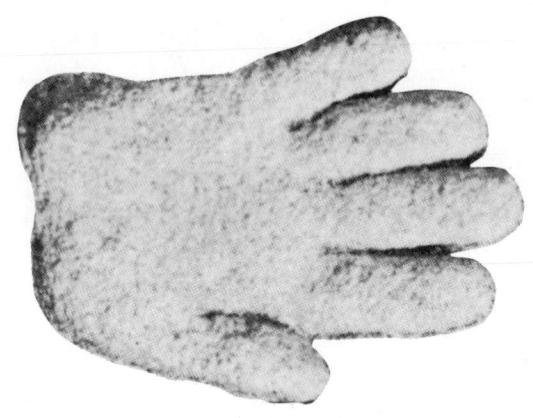

16 *Sand*

FLOWER POT

Tools: Paste jar or cold cream jar, pencil or nail, top of ink bottle or bottle cap, box (any small box will do).

1. Press the jar into the wet sand.
Dig the top portion of the jar deeper into the sand than the lower portion.

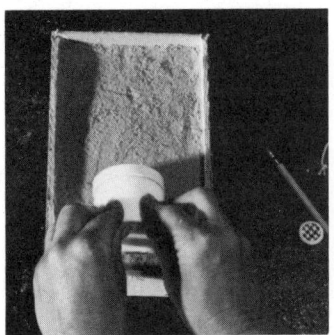 

2. Make a curved line with the pencil or nail for the stalk.

3. Press the top of the bottle cap into the sand to make the flower petals.

4. Use the open or screw-end of the bottle cap to make the center of the flower.

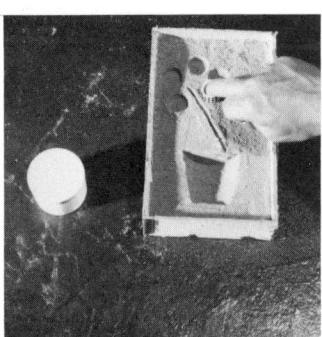 

5. Draw leaves with the pencil or nail, digging gently into the sand.

6. Mix the plaster, dribble and pour it, then place your hook. Let the cast dry, turn it out and brush.

With the same basic design you can get many different and interesting sculptures.

For instance, instead of using a bottle cap to make the flower petals, you can use shells or bits of colored glass. Press the shells or bits of glass into the wet sand. Don't press them in too deeply.

In the photograph below right, colored bits of glass that had been found on the beach were used. The sea had smoothed and polished them.

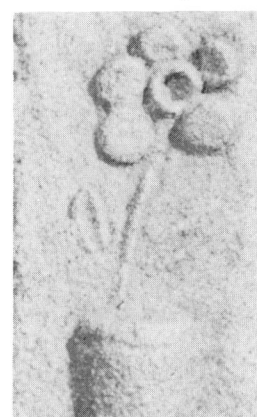 

HOUSE

Tools: Wood block, ruler, small square bottle or square of wood, box.

Press the wood block into the sand, leaving ½ inch of space at the bottom edge of the box. Hold the wood block vertically and make four imprints, one right next to each other. Be sure your imprints are even in depth. Now make one deeper impression on the right-hand side of the first impression.

2. Leave ½ inch of space above the bottom impression. Turn the wood block (as shown in the photograph) and press it into the sand evenly, one right next to the other.

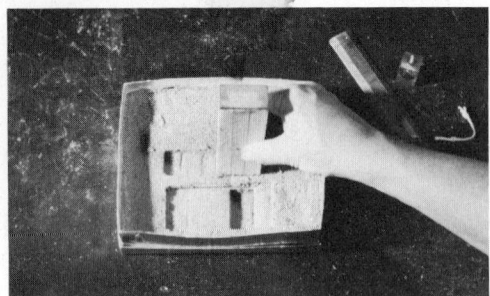

3. Press a bottle or wood square into the sand in the center of the box above the other imprints. Use the same small square to make an impression in the left-hand corner of the bottom, or first, impression.

4. Using your ruler, dig two lines above the square to form a V. Dig two short lines into the sand above the right-hand line.

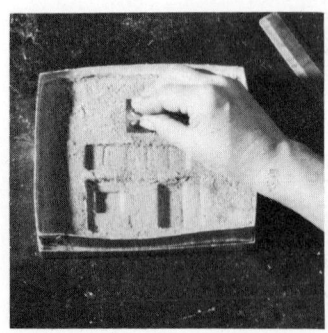 

5. Dig several straight lines with a pencil into the center impression.
   Mix the plaster, dribble and pour it, then place your hook. Let the cast dry, turn it out and brush.

BIRD IN TREE

Tools: Nail file, twig from bush, hedge, or tree, small wooden bird, box.

1. Place the twig so that it looks like the trunk of a tree. Press gently into the wet sand.

2. With the point of a nail file dig into the sand to make the leaves of the tree. Don't dig too deeply.

3. Place the wooden bird on the branch. Press into sand. Make a line for the horizon with the point of the nail file.

4. Mix the plaster, dribble and pour it, then place your hook. Let the cast dry, turn it out and brush.

18 *Sand*

HORSES

Any object that has shape or form will make an impression in wet sand. If you have a favorite little figurine—a china dog, a bronze cat, or a wooden doll—that you would like to use for a mold, you can do so. Here is a sand sculpture in which a pottery horse was used for the design.

Tools: Pottery horse, pencil, box.

Press the head of the pottery horse into the wet sand on one side of the box. Repeat this twice, making one impression deeper than the other two.

Draw these letters on the other side of your sculpture, being sure not to dig too deeply.

Mix the plaster, dribble and pour it, then place your hook. Let the cast dry, turn it out and brush.

This sand sculpture looks like an old fragment you might find in a museum.

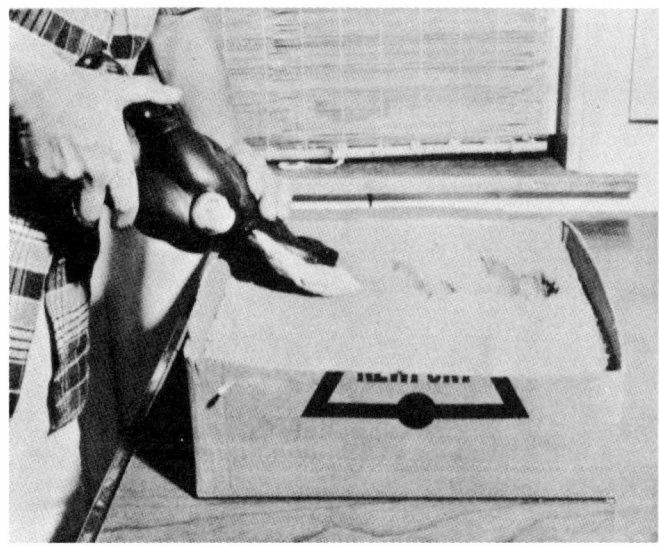

Using the pencil, make letters that are similar to ancient writing—Egyptian or Persian or Chinese.

ABSTRACT

Some of the most interesting sculptures are abstracts. These are designs or compositions that do not necessarily depict anything realistic. They are interesting because they have form, composition, and varying depths that give light and dark effects.

In sand sculpture you can scoop out sand to make your design. Instead of pressing a tool into the wet sand, you scoop the sand out. The following simple abstract will show you how to scoop a design.

Tools: Small spatula or plasterer's scraper, small glass or small jam jar, box.

1. Scoop out an area in the upper left-hand corner. Be sure your edges are clean and straight.

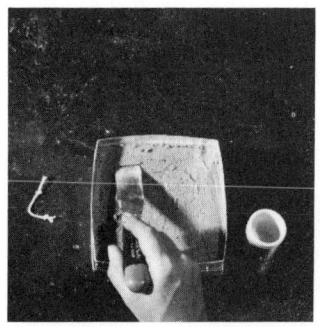 

Sand 19

2. Scoop out an area on the left-hand side of the box. This should be deeper than the area in step 1; see the photograph on page 19.

3. Scoop out the sand on the right-hand side of the box directly opposite the area of step 2.

4. Scoop out the sand at the bottom of the box.

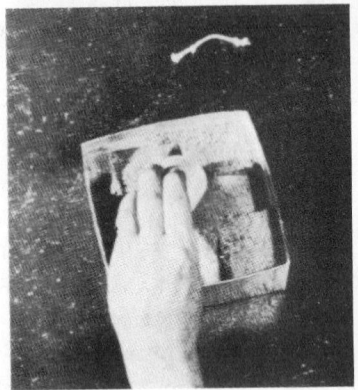 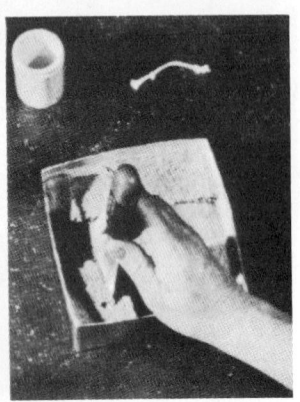  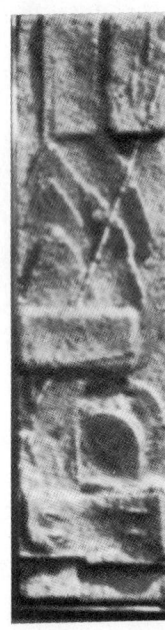

5. Press the bottom of a small glass or jar to make semicircles in the center of the box. Press first impression deeper than next two.

6. With your spatula make a cross in the bottom, right-hand corner of the sand. Dig two lines in the bottom, left-hand corner.

Mix the plaster, dribble and pour it, then place your hook. Let the cast dry, turn it out and brush.

Have you remembered to insert your picture hook? You didn't? Well, don't worry. Your sand sculpture can be displayed resting on a plate stand. You can buy a plate stand made of wire in a dime store, or in hardware stores or gift shops.

You may also mount your sculpture on a piece of wood. Simply put two hooks and a picture wire on the back of the wood and then glue the sculpture to the front of the wood.

In the beginning of this book I promised to tell you how to do sand sculpture at the beach. You do not need a worktable at the beach. You work directly in the sand. Instead of using a box for your mold, all you need are four pieces of wood—driftwood or any old wood you can find to make your mold. Your materials are the same. You need sand, and you have miles of it all around you. You need plaster, a pail or bucket, a piece of cord, a brush, and water. You have an oceanful of the last item. Your tools may be beach toys, wood, shells, a shovel, rocks, your hands and feet. Again, anything that will make an impression in wet sand.

20 *Sand*

The sculptures are made exactly the same way that you make them at home or at school. The one main difference is that you do not have to worry about digging too deeply. You can dig your design as deeply as you wish, and you will get some exciting effects.

Your mold is exactly as it is at home or at school. However, if the day is bright and sunny (and it generally is when one spends a day at the beach), your mold will be ready to turn out in fifteen or twenty minutes. In turning out your mold, instead of breaking or peeling your box away from the mold, all you do is carefully lift out one piece of wood at a time. Turn out your mold. Let it dry for ten minutes and then brush.

In doing more advanced work, whether at the beach, home, or at school, the method is always the same. Just press or scoop in wet sand to get your design.

Have you noticed that when you dig a line in the sand on the left-hand side of the box, the line appears on the right-hand side when your mold has been cast and turned out? That is because you are always doing your design in reverse.

For instance, if you want to sign your sculpture and your name is Jean, you would have to write your letters backwards like this: Write your name on a slip of paper and look at it in a mirror and that is what you would see.

When you are ready to do a more advanced sand sculpture and you have decided on your composition or sketched a design for your composition on paper, you must remember to work in reverse. That is, if you want a square, for example, to appear on the right-hand corner of your sculpture, you must scoop or press it in on the left corner. If you have a stone or a shell that you want to be in the left-hand corner of your sculpture, you must place it in the right-hand corner as you work.

Varying the depths in your sculpture will give you better effects. You will have more "interest" in your piece, more lights and shadows. Your composition will have character and not be just a dull plaque.

Here are photographs of two sculptures. One is shallow, and one has depths and shallows, hills and valleys. The second sculpture is the "stronger" of the two.

In doing larger pieces we follow the same simple directions as for small pieces. We choose a larger box, we impress our design as we did for the small molds, and we mix our plaster in the same way. There is one important difference in pouring our plaster. After dribbling the first layer from our fingers onto the sand, take pieces of florist wire and place it on the plaster. Then pour the remaining plaster over the crisscrossed wire reinforcement.

 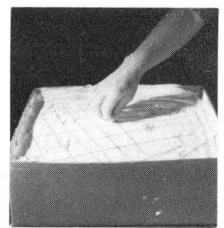 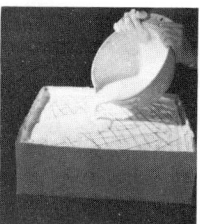

The wire reinforces the mold so that it will be strong and not break when it is turned out. Small molds can be reinforced in the same fashion for extra strength. Chicken mesh can be used in place of florist wire.

When making the "picture hook" for the large sand sculptures, wrap a piece of florist wire around the cord for extra strength.

The large sculpture can also be mounted on a block of wood by gluing it to a wooden board with any strong adhesive product.

The following are photographs of small and large pieces that I have done. The same ready-to-find tools were used in making them. The only bought tool is a plasterer's scraper, which can be purchased in any paint shop.

The world is as full of objects as ideas. You can make sand sculptures that are not only exciting and decorative but artistic as well. Sand sculpture is an old and simple art form, but it is an art nonetheless. Perhaps you won't turn out museum pieces, but you can turn out molds that will make any room more attractive.

Slate Sculpturing

A blackboard reminds one of chalk, an eraser, and a schoolroom. Flagstone makes one think of garden walks or patios. But after you have read this book and done some carvings, you will never look at a piece of slate again without thinking what a fine wall plaque could be made from it.

Blackboards are made of slate. Slate has a hard surface, but it is a surprisingly soft material to work. You can get slate and flagstone (flagstone is usually thicker) at any building supply house. They often have broken pieces that they are happy to give away. Do not use flags made of blue stone, however, for they have a hard surface that is difficult to work.

A fragment of slate (14" x 4") that had been thrown on the rubbish heap suggested a fish to the artist. Below is a picture of the result.

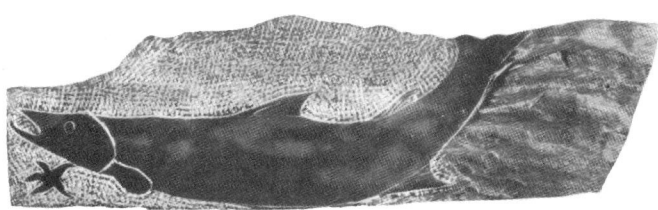

You can also buy blackboards in toy shops, stationery stores, and dime stores. Small ones are quite inexpensive.

The nice thing about slate is that you need not know how to draw. Your design can be traced onto the slate. If you are a budding artist and want to do an original piece, all you do is draw a design or figure on

the slate in chalk. Chalk is wonderful to work with, because if you wish to make any changes, you can erase or correct your design until you get a composition that pleases you.

Professional artists use special tools for carving. You will read about these later in the book, but since, in the beginning, the objective is to show you not only how to make an attractive carving but how to make it easily, you will use only a nail and a screw driver. These tools can be found in almost every home.

The following pages will give you step-by-step directions for simple carvings.

MATERIALS

You will need a piece of slate or flagstone, a nail, screw driver, sandpaper (very fine) or emery cloth, paste wax (or floor wax, automobile wax, etc.), chalk or tracing and carbon paper, a pencil and a rag.

Have your materials ready. A table, desk, or any flat surface makes a good workbench.

1. Before starting the first piece, let us experiment. Select a piece of slate. Draw an oval on the slate with chalk. Using a nail about 2½" in length, scratch or "incise" the outline of the oval; see the photograph on the next page.

23

2. If you find working with the nail hard on your hand, you can wrap a piece of adhesive or any sticky tape around the middle of the nail to act as a cushion.

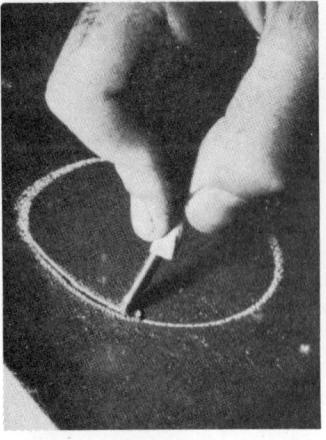 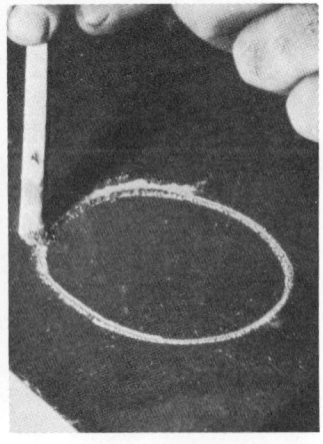

3. Now take the screw driver and scrape or dig around the outside of the oval, removing a thin layer of slate in order to make the oval stand out. The slate you remove looks like gray dust. The untouched area or figure then seems to leap forward.

4. With the nail, dig several holes into the oval for a polka-dotted effect.

 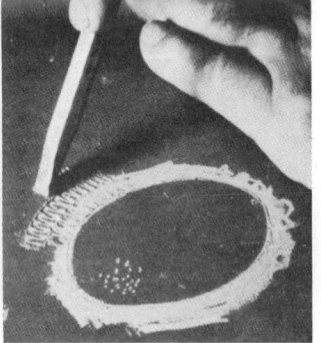

5. Using the screw driver, roll your wrist back and forth to make the screw driver "walk." This gives a textured rather than a flat effect for the background.

Keep your hands in back of your work to prevent injury if a tool should slip. This is very important to remember.

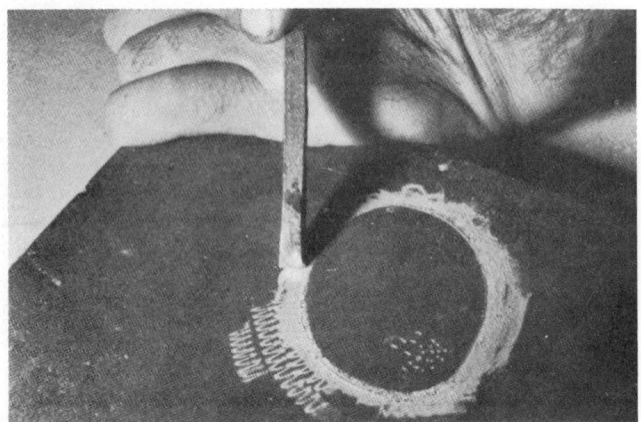

TRACING

If you don't want to draw your *own* design, you can trace one.

Select a picture you would like to duplicate. Place a piece of tracing paper over the picture. Follow the outline of the picture lightly with a pencil. See *pages 30–31* for drawings you can trace.

Place a piece of carbon paper, shiny side down, on the piece of slate you have chosen to carve. Place the tracing paper over the carbon. Go over the outline of the picture with a pencil, pressing a little harder so that your design will appear clearly on the slate. The slate is now ready to be worked.

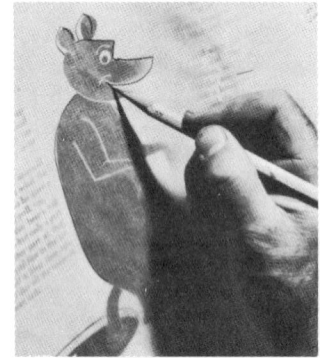 

SIMPLE SCULPTURE

Now that you know some of the tricks of slate sculpturing, here is a simple one to start with.

BIRD

Trace or draw a bird on slate. See *page 30* for a sample drawing. The artist used a piece that measured 5" x 5" for his carving, but any small piece will do.

1. Scratch or incise the outline of the bird with the nail.

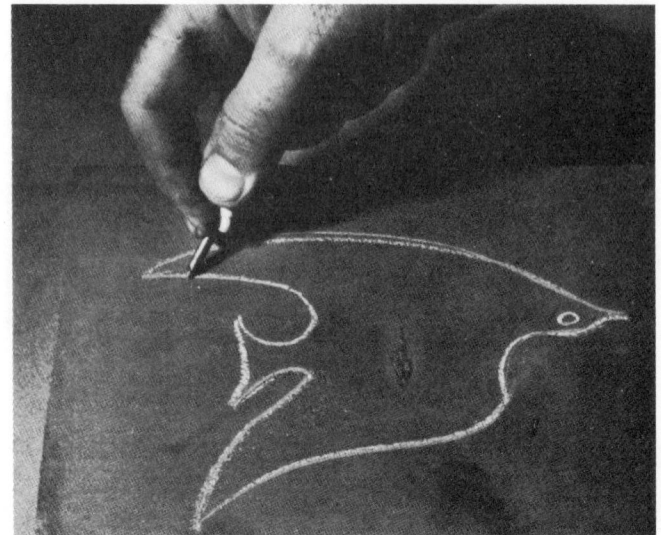

24 *Slate*

2. Dig out the background with the screw driver.

3. Sandpaper only those surfaces that are to be waxed and polished. This is to smooth away any roughness and remove any scratches so that your figure will take on a high polish and reflect the light. In this case, only sandpaper the bird.

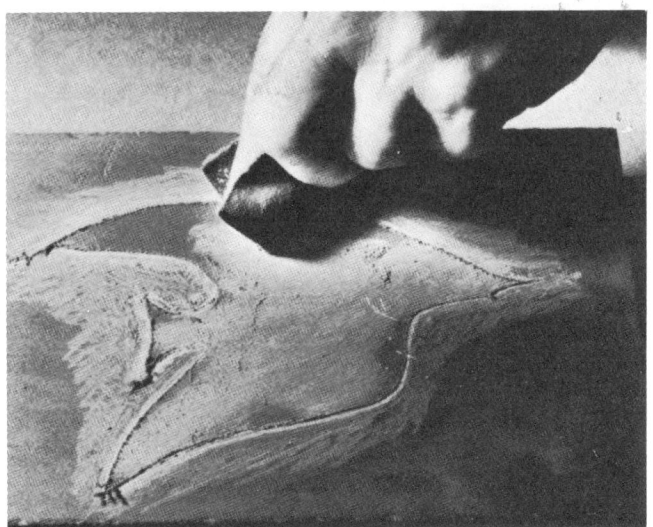

4. Make the eye of the bird with the nail.

5. Apply wax to areas you wish to have stand out. Then polish with a soft cloth.

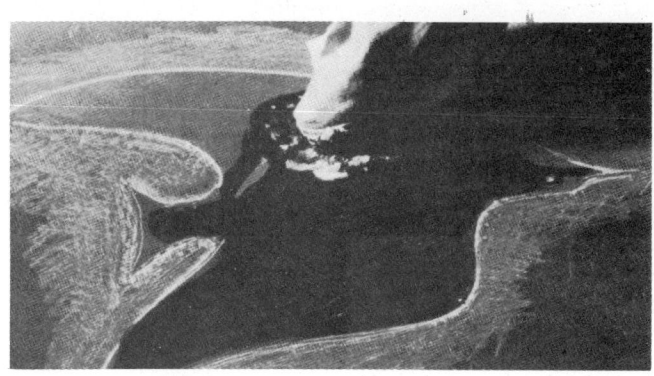

6. Use the nail to dig the wax from the outlines of your figure.

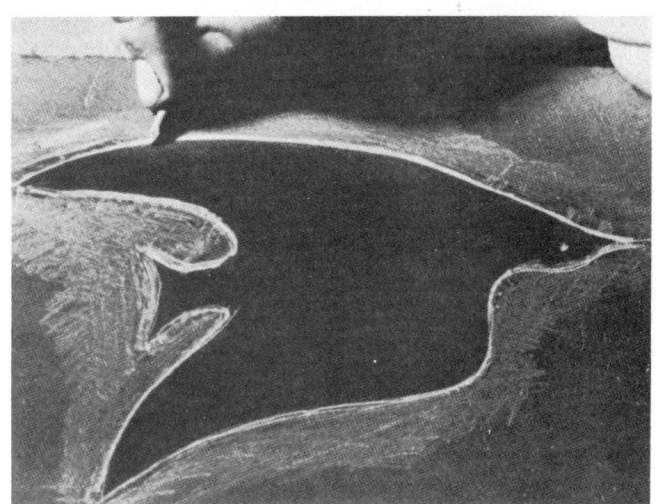

The bird slate is now completed.

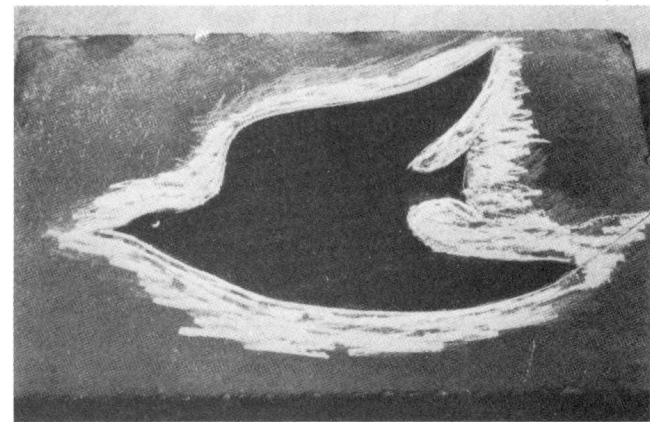

Slate 25

SAILBOAT

Draw or trace a sailboat. See *page 31* for a sample drawing.

1. Scratch or incise the outline of the sailboat with the nail.

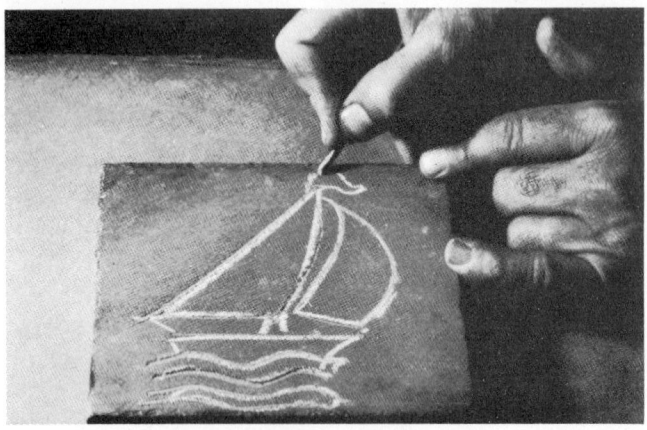

2. Texture the background by "walking" the screw driver.

3. Sandpaper all surfaces that are to stand out. Wax only the boat, waves, and pennant. Polish. Remove the wax from the lines with the nail. Polish again.

ROUNDED SCULPTURE

In order to get a more rounded sculpture one has to carve inside the figure or design to contrast low and high areas. The following carving will show you how this is done.

HORSE

Trace or draw a horse's head on slate. See *page 31* for a sample drawing. The piece used here measures 8″ x 13″. Scratch the outline with the nail.

1. Carve muscles in the horse's neck with the screw driver.

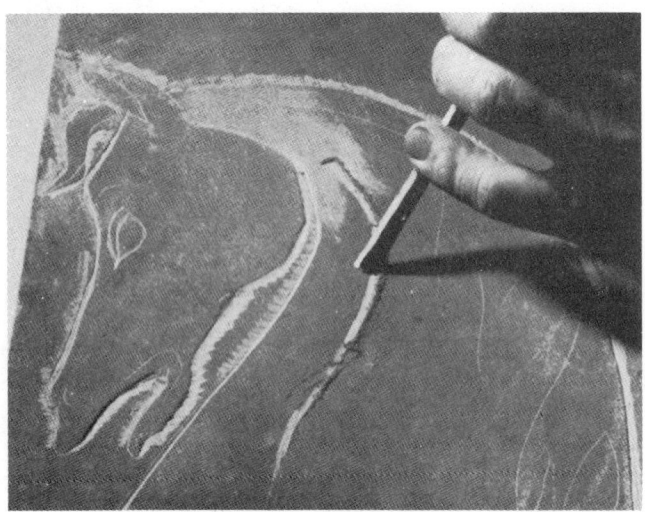

2. Carve low areas for the horse's eye, ear, and cheek.

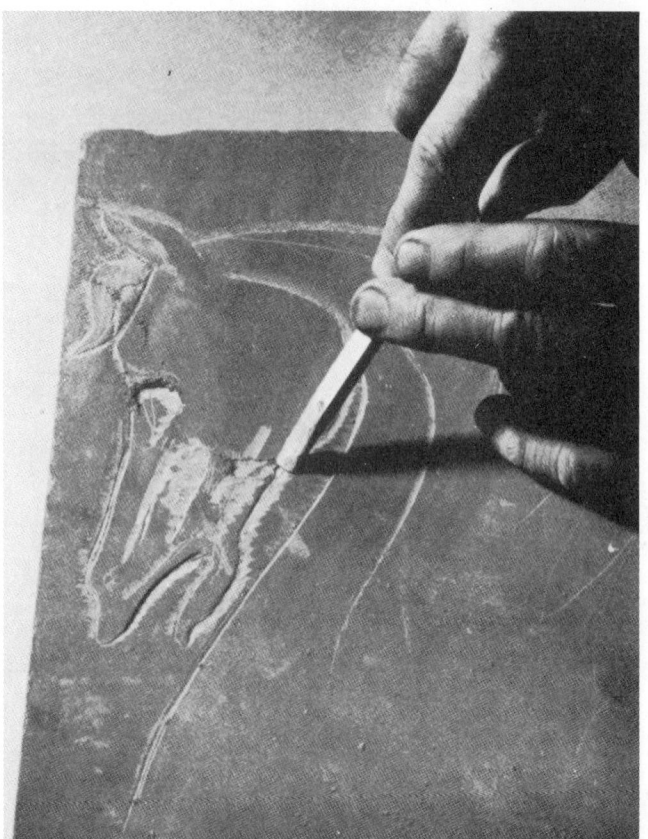

26 *Slate*

3. Walk the screw driver for a textured background. Sandpaper the surfaces to be waxed and polished. Redefine the outline of the head with the nail. Polish with a soft cloth.

Besides rounding forms in slate to get a more effective sculpture, one can also add additional design by rubbing dry colors or gold and bronze powders into the lines that have been scratched out with the nail. These powders should be mixed with a little shellac (just enough to make the mixture opaque, not translucent and watery) before applying. They can be purchased at any paint or art store.

The same steps used before should be followed in making the Indian head pictured below. However, when the carving is finished, rub gold powder into the features. Then wax and polish.

SHAPING SLATE

As was mentioned earlier in the book, slate is an extremely easy medium to work with. It not only can be carved, but it can be sawed as well.

This sliver of slate, 12" x 4", was carved and shaped into a whale.

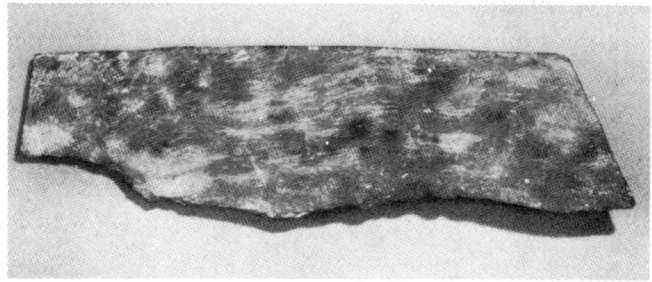

WHALE

1. Draw or trace a whale on slate. See *page 31* for a sample drawing.

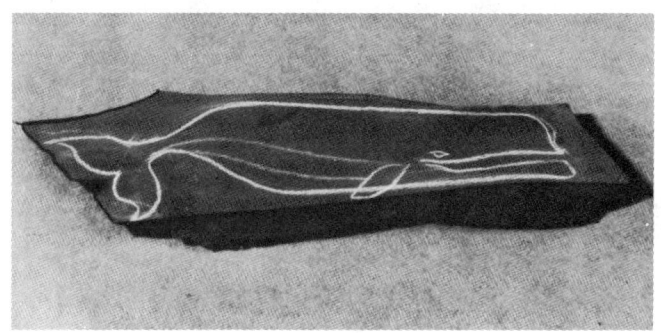

2. Incise or scratch the outline. Carefully shape the outline of the tail on the whale with a hack saw or a jig saw.

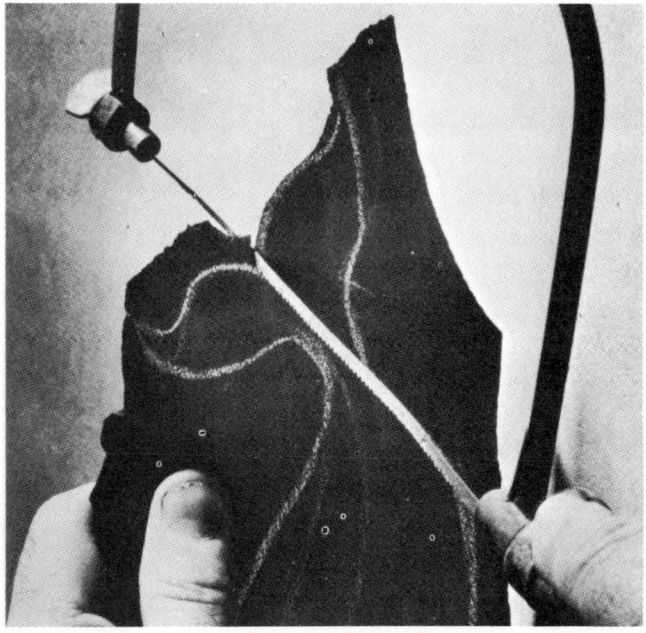

Slate 27

3. If you make a mistake and accidentally break a piece of slate, don't worry, for you can change the shape of the design.

4. Smooth the rough edges with sandpaper.

5. For a rounded effect carve the edges of the tail with a screw driver.

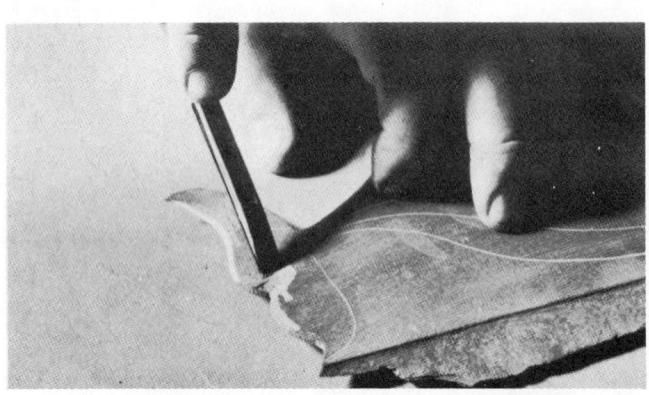

6. Using the nail, outline all parts that are to stand out. Walk the screw driver for a textured background.

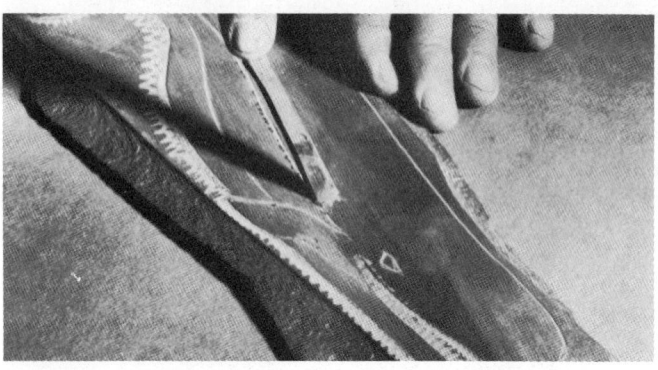

7. Sandpaper the surfaces that are to be waxed and polished. Apply wax. Polish with a soft cloth.

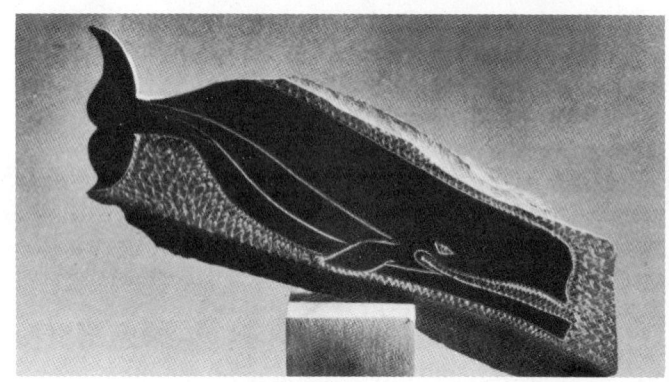

ABSTRACTS

28 *Slate*

Abstracts make handsome and original slate carvings. An abstract is a design or composition that does not necessarily depict anything realistic. They are interesting because they have form, composition, and varying depths that give light and dark effects.

Draw two triangles or a cube and a circle or a square and a circle, etc. Incise your outline with the nail. Walk, scrape, or dig the screw driver to create a background and low areas and see what an attractive piece you can come up with.

The simple abstract was done by the artist on a small piece of slate, 3″ x 8″.

DISPLAY

When a slate sculpture is finished, it is ready to be displayed. Here are three simple ways to hang or show your work.

1. Make a groove with a saw the same thickness as the slate in a block of wood. Slide the sculpture into the groove.

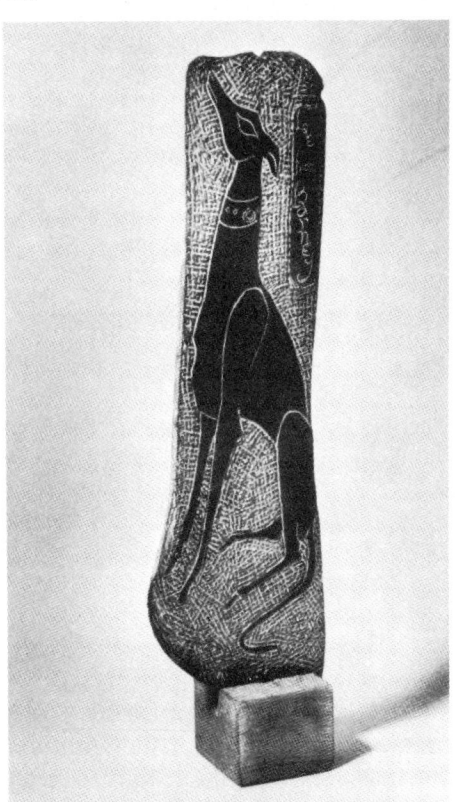

3. Make a hole in your sculpture by slowly drilling into the slate with a hand drill. Put picture wire through the hole and hang the sculpture on a wall from a picture hook.

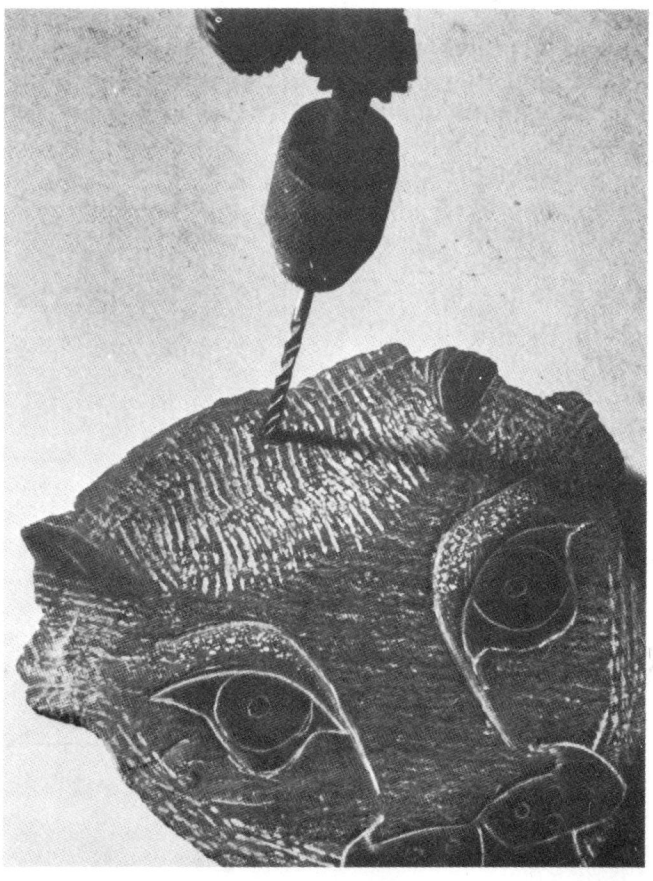

2. Holding the slate sculpture against a wall, mark dots on the wall with a pencil on the top and the bottom of the sculpture. Remove the slate and drive nails into these dots on the wall. Hang your sculpture by bending the nails slightly around it to hold it securely.

Slate 29

ADVANCED TECHNIQUES

Professional sculptors work slate in any size. When using large pieces of slate or flagstone, it is advisable to use a clamp to hold the slate in place. A clamp should be used whenever you are working a piece that doesn't lie flat, no matter what its size. Slate sculpturing requires a firm base on which to work. If slate slips around, you can make mistakes.

The more advanced sculptors use the following tools for carving.

Scriber: A pointed instrument with a rubber handle. The type used to scribe leather is best for working slate. However, an awl or the nail we have been speaking about throughout the book work equally as well. The scriber is preferable only because it is made of tempered steel and stays sharper longer.

Rasp or riffler: A kind of file, which is often curved. This tool is used to deepen the lines scratched with the scriber or nail. The rasp is pushed forward slowly and with a steady pressure. A slight rolling of the wrist makes it work more easily.

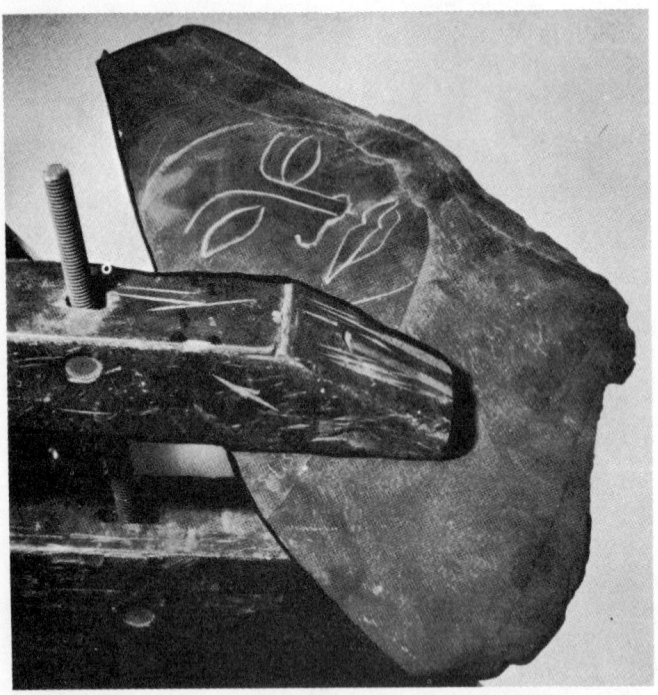

Toothed chisel: A chisel on which the cutting edge is toothed rather than smooth. This tool is used for texturing large surfaces. A screw driver into which teeth have been filed is just as good. The toothed chisel is used to crosshatch the background and gives greater contrast to the waxed and polished raised figures.

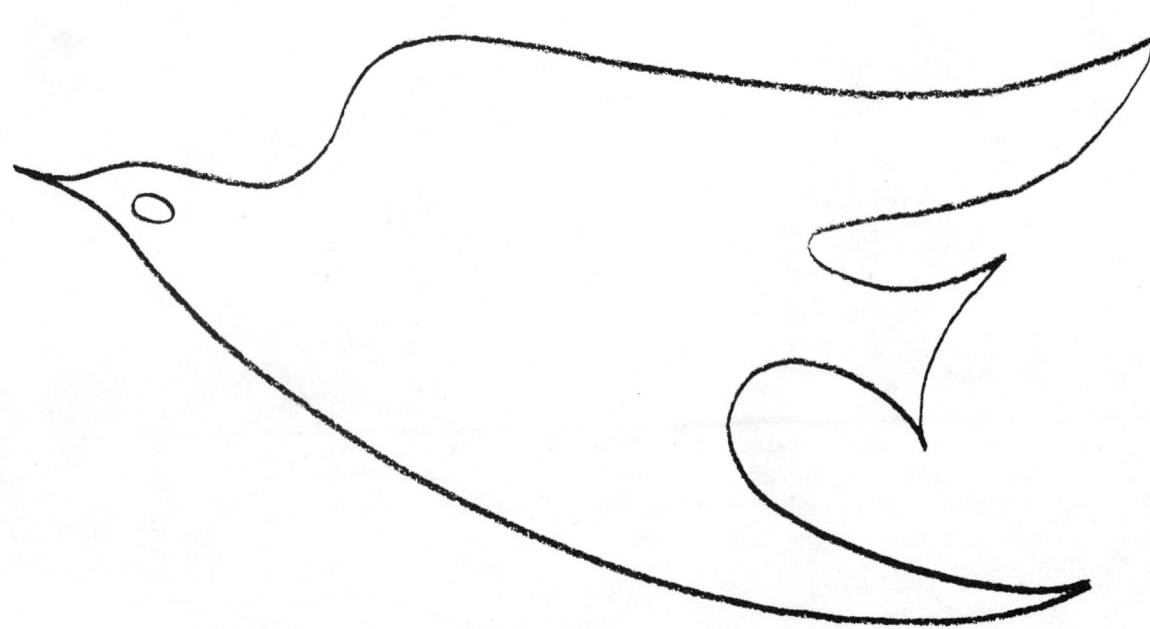

30 *Slate*

Slate 31